The Power of Positive Thinking to Create Wealth

By Anthony DeMarco

Why Creating Wealth Seems Difficult

There are many reasons which lead people to not to be rich. Try to think over about yourself and find which factor that affects you then start to make a change. These are some factors that hinder people to be rich:

1. Wrong or Colluding Believes:

The first factor that can explain why many people are not rich is the wrong believes about wealth and the colluding believes between negative and positive believes.

Basically, human's brain always tries to find pleasure and avoid suffer. If something is related to hardship, we'll tend to avoid it. In the other way, if something has a strong relationship with pleasure we'll get closer to it. If something is associated to pleasure and hardship, our brain will be confused or neutral. Believes is just like magnet. If positive belief is mixed up with the negative ones, there is no more "positive polar" or "negative polar." Our minds will be neutral or confused as regular metal. When we are sure that "being rich" is positive, while "being poor" is negative, the pole will be much clearer, thus we'll become a "magnet."

In fact, many people never set his belief consciously from birth to death. If we do not establish our own conscious beliefs of the need to be rich, without realizing we will be carried away by words such as "Money is the root of all evil deeds".

At the results, unconsciously we don't want to be rich because we do not want to be evil. For example: James has a friend who is very wealthy and has a very large house and magnificent. Charles and Mary went to visit their friend James. As they arrive at James' house, Charles asked Mary "Isn't the house nice?" Mary then replied; "I do not like big house, because it'll be difficult to clean it," then Charles said: "If you got a big and magnificent house like this, it's impossible to clean it yourself". The above example shows that Mary has false belief, each time she saw great house she would be stressed as she thought it would be troublesome to clean.

2. Unclear Objectives:

The second reason why we are not rich is because we never set purpose or goal, or we continue to change our purpose thus it is become unclear. It's important for us to set goals, since without purpose our movement will be entirely aimless. Example: When you get out of the house and then you stop a taxi. After that, the driver would ask "Where are you going" and you say "Whatever". There are two possibilities that will happen, the first driver will take you around the city and then drive you back to your home. The second, driver will bring you then take you to somewhere that you do not like. The same happens in life. If you do not specify exactly what the purpose of your life then you will waste time, energy and money. You will have difficulty pursuing your goals. Furthermore, a lot of people unconsciously or consciously keep changing its target before the target is reached.

3. Considering the Objective as Impossible:

It's sad that only very few people who dare to set a life goal. Even worse, they are considering their life goal impossible. In establishing the purpose of our life, we should be very personal or private. We can't just follow what others do. It's okay if others thinking that our goals are impossible, but ourselves are unsure of our own goal. Once you think that your goal is impossible, and then you will not do anything to pursue your goals. You will become more like lazy, indecisive, and not serious and do not have the spirit.

Clearly results would not be satisfactory. Humans tend to do something with his. So, when his beliefs say that the goal is impossible, then what he does will be weak and not good?

4. Do Not Feel Compelled:

When we set goals, but we feel that there is no strong urge to achieve it although we can achieve these objectives, we are not motivated to achieve it. It's caused by the absence of necessity. If we do not feel something as a necessity from within ourselves, small obstacles are enough to stop our efforts to achieve that goal. For example: Although you have determined that the following year you want to buy a Jaguar car but if you do not feel it as a must then you won't ever buy the car. Even though you have lots of money to buy it, you still won't buy it. 5. Do not have a strategy that proved successful Although we already have the right belief, the right purpose, and feel the need, but if the strategy is wrong, we still won't reach our goal. For example: photography has the goal to take photograph of the sunrise. Naturally, the sun will rise from the east direction, but the photographer keeps walking to the west. At any given time, he will not be able to photograph the sunrise.

6. Not knowing the path of natural or easiest to achieve goals Such as nuts

and bolts that don't fit together will be useless. When the nut is too small no matter how hard we try, the efforts seem futile. Indeed, we can try to push bolts that are too small into the nut, but it takes more effort and we often do not enjoy the process or even the results.

7. Don't have a realistic plan Having a purpose without any realistic plan would be troublesome to execute the plan. Thus, we will have difficulty in achieving the goal.

8. Do not act in accordance with the plan Another mistake is that often the person is tempted to come out of the original plan. It is true that we need to change our plan if the plan proves to take us further from our original purpose. But in the other hand, if the

plan is already established and lead us the right way, we need to be consistent in doing our plan to pursue our defined purpose. 9. Not observing and measuring the next mistake that leads people to not to be rich is that people often doesn't not keep track of the process, whether it is aiming to the purpose or not. People taking action as the already planned, but most of the time they don't want to keep track or measure how far have they got. In business, we must measure and monitor our business progress once a month at the minimum.

10. Putting the responsibility to others When someone starts blaming other people, blaming economic factors, blamed the situation, this person will

not learn from failure. Those who do not learn from its failures are people who fail indeed. The greatest weakness of people who blame everything was that that a person felt that she or he was right and did not need to act again. When someone starts to make excuses like saying too young, too old, just graduated from junior high school, not talented, I'm a woman, I'm the man, I just ... I too ... I do not ..., etc... People like this will not act at all. And if there is no action, there will be no result whatsoever. Self-justification is an attempt to cover up the weakness or lack of motivation to change for the better by justifying the circumstances as something natural or given. Example: "It is sure that I cannot work since I do not have a degree! It is not surprising at all that Andy always get the promotion because he was overseas graduates!" When looking at other people who are more powerful than themselves that kind of people will justify without inspired to learn or become stronger. They prefer to use expressions like "Of course ...", "Of course ...", "It Properly ..."

11. Easy to give up Many people experienced something like someone digging for gold. They stopped digging the gold digging 30 cm before the spade hitting the gold.

12. Do not manage your life as a business that should be profitable Every year there is no improvement in life. Therefore, life will be useless as nothing is produced. If a business in a few years

results no profits, the business will be closed. We cannot use the excuse that because the operational cost is large, the revenue can only be used to cover operating costs. Results of operations should be greater than all costs. As well as in life, even just a little we should make profit every year.

13. Influenced by pessimism and optimism of others When we are affected by another person, even if that person is included in 5% of people who own 90% of the money circulation, we are in conditions less favorable. It is caused by the unavailability of our own system. Maybe we will win at a time, but we don't know why we win. This will lead to optimism without a foundation

and will result in the following fatal defeat.

14. Have a good mentor If we try to try everything in this life on our own, we will spend the time and energy more than if we could learn from people who are already successful in the field that we want. Many people ask to 95% of people on average, thus the result will be the average. If we want to succeed, we have to ask the best 5% or to 1% of the best, who are above average and listen to their advice.

Financial Freedom

What does it mean to be rich? Some people consider themselves rich when they have ten million dollars, while others don't think the same way. According to Forbes magazine, rich people are those who have income of at least US $ 1 million per year. While referring to Robert T. Kiyosaki, rich people are not measured by how much active income is, but the so-called rich if someone's passive income is greater than the cost of living. What is meant here passive income is money that comes without working.

According to Anthony Robbins, the rich are divided into 6 stages.

1. Financial Protection is a financial condition where we have enough money to meet monthly spending minimum, for 2 months to 24 months without having to work.

2. Financial Security is a condition of the financial where we have quite a lot of investment is relatively safe and the results can meet these needs without having to work again, unless we choose to work. Life necessities for example home installments, the cost of food, electricity, gas, water, transportation, insurance and taxes.

3. Financial Vitality is a financial condition where we have quite a lot of investment, that is relatively safe, and the results are not only able to meet the needs at the level of Financial Security.

Furthermore, it can make us choose to work or not. Life necessities for example education of children, holiday needs, buying new clothes or to have two luxury items that make sense.

4. Financial Independence is a financial condition where we achieved quite a lot of investment that is relatively safe and the results are sufficient for us to live exactly with our present lifestyle, without having to work again for the rest of our lives. In other words, we are free from working.

5. Financial Freedom is a financial condition where we achieved quite a lot of investment that is relatively safe and the results are sufficient for us to live a lifestyle that we want.

6. Absolute Financial Freedom is a financial condition where we achieved quite a lot of investment is relatively safe and therefore we are confident that we can make real whatever we want, whenever we want, wherever we want, with anyone we want, as much and as we want in a way that makes us and others powerless forever. Rich simply means to have passive income is greater than the lifestyle that we want. How to become rich quickly and safely:

1. Have the right and strong determination to become rich.

2. Determine clear and steady goals.

3. Convinced that he himself can achieve the goal.

4. Feel the need to reach the goal.

5. Having proven strategies that help he himself to be rich quickly and safely.

6. Knowing and using natural and easy path for himself.

7. Make a realistic plan.

8. Take actions in accordance with the plan.

9. Conduct monitoring and being sensitive.

10. Responsible for continuous learning and acting.

Determination to Be Rich

What is determination? Determination is something we believe in and live within us, which consciously or unconsciously determine our attitudes and actions. Such beliefs can be tangible, such as "rule or law stating causal laws" that lives in the hearts or our minds.

Example: 1. When my proposal was rejected three times, I do not need to propose anymore.

2. If I want to be rich, then I will work hard.

3. If I do not sleep, then I will be sluggish.

4. If you do not have a college degree, then don't expect to be manager.

Deliberately here the arrangement of "If ..., then ..." are affirmed although these are grammatically incorrect. In another form, "rules of the heart" can be like:

1. If three of my friends who are smarter than me just failed to run a business, how could I be successful?

2. My family is not a merchant; it is not surprising that I don't fit in marketing. The belief here can also mean "identity" or "global formula of something" or "statements about something" that lives in the hearts or our minds and influencing our attitudes and actions.

Example: 1. Life is a struggle.

2. Money is the source of all problems.

3. I am a person who is not talented to be salesman.

4. I am a lucky man the importance of a right belief Determination can make people sick, can make people die, can make people kill people, can make people poor or even can make people rich. Oftentimes we do not know where this belief came from and probably already embedded in our subconscious. Maybe we just heard and logically we do not really care, but because our subconscious is affected then the belief becomes conviction for us. In campus Mary was teasing Anto, she suddenly asked him "Anto, why you look really pale?" A few moments later during learning process, suddenly a lecturer asked Anto "Anto, why your face look

pale?" The next day Anto did not go to college because of sick. Mary who visited him in his house said "Anto, actually yesterday I was only joking by saying your face was very pale, but surprisingly you are actually ill now." The above example demonstrates that anything that comes into us and we believe will have tremendous force to change us. Therefore, we need to be selective and only belief the things that support us in our belief system. The human brain is like a magnet, if our beliefs about money are opposite to each other, unconsciously we will stay away from money or become neutral towards money. Therefore, to become rich we mustchange our negative beliefs about money into positive ones.

Where do beliefs come from? Beliefs come from the experience that we read, hear feel, both consciously and unconsciously. That belief underlies the way we think, speak and act in the present and in the future. Often what we believe becomes actual reality for us. Our beliefs influence our actions, and then our actions will affect the potential that we use. Further, our potential will affect the results that we want and the results obtained will bring influence into our confidence. The stronger the results, the greater our confidence and vice versa. Some people feel gifted or not gifted about something, such as mathematics. Does the brain and body are different? Generally, the answer is no. Sometimes what happens is that someone feels not gifted because of its small failure experiences in the past.

Example: A child has not taught the concept of numbers 1,2, 3 when entering a school. In the other sides, his friends are able and master the concept of numbers. Perhaps the teacher couldn't teach in the right way, and shortly the child only scores 2 out of 10 on exams. What happen next? Because the results are considered bad, in the future the child may conclude that he is not gifted mathematics. Due to his conclusion that he is not gifted in math, when he has mathematics test he was lazing so that the results are very bad.

Another example is about Adam Khoo. At the age of 26, he has four businesses which have a turnover until $ 20 million.

When he was only 12 years old, Adam was known as a lazy, stupid, mildly retarded and a hopeless boy. When he entered elementary-school he hated reading and only wanted to play games and watch TV. He always got bad scores at school. He hated his teacher and his school. He got the lowest ranking, that's why his parents panicked and sent him to a lot of courses. It turned out that those things didn't help much. At the age of 13, Adam Khoo was sent to a special school that uses NLP technology.

Since then, he changed and had determination that he could be successful. There, he was taught to think positive, about good character building, and building thought to be rich people. Since that moment, he changed completely. In the first testing he got an A. Henceforth, he continued to be a nice person and his parents are very happy. The above examples that mind can easily change our lives. The Right Belief Can Increase Luck There was study in the UK that is conducted to 1,000 people. Those people had previously been surveyed and divided into two groups: one group of people who are very lucky and the other group consisted of people who are very disadvantaged. Then, everyone was asked to buy a lottery ticket. From 700 participants in the lottery, here is the following result: 36 people win and half of them come from the lucky group while the other 18 people were from very unlucky group.

From the 36 people, there are two individuals who managed to guess 4 numbers correctly, one of them come from the very lucky group, while the other is from very unlucky group. This survey proved that lucky or not lucky depends on the right and wrong beliefs. From this moment if there come negative thoughts in our brain, we must immediately say "cancel" or "nonsense" and then proceed with positive beliefs or words. Using affirmation Affirmations are one sentence with strong emotions and you start to believe it. It can also be combined with moves such as "My day is getting stronger" while stiffen your muscles. Examples of affirmations:

1. No matter what happens, I am getting stronger and stronger.

2. All that I need to succeed is already in me.

3. Every day I grow a healthy, wealthy and happy. Repeat your affirmations every morning coupled with movement.

Clear Goals

Activities are not the same as the productivity. In life, people often don't realize whether they are doing an activity or productivity. We often get stuck in the activity without making any productivity because we did not define a clear purpose in our lives.

The principle in determining objectives:

1. It should be positive words.

2. Specific.

3. Written Goals Should be Formulated Positively Purpose or goal should be formulated in positive words because our subconscious mind doesn't recognize the word "no". What happened when a person has a purpose in the negative words, such as "I do not

want to be poor and do not want to fail"? The person will become poor and failed. Examples of positive words in setting goals:

1. Joyfully and happily, I (write your name) already have income (daily amount) per month, since the date of (write the date you want).

2. Joyfully and pleasure and tremendous spirit, I've moved into my new house with an area of (write area you want) at (write your desired location) since (write the date you want). Goals Should be Specific When you do not want to say: "tomorrow I wake up at 5 am" and it turns out that the next morning you wake up on time according to your wishes.

It can happen because during sleep our subconscious mind keeps working. Our subconscious always pursues the goal and won't deny a specific, clear and steady purpose. Example: At a seminar, a speaker asked all students who participated in the seminar on "Who wants to be richer than now? Step forward". And dozens of people came forward, then the speaker gives each student as much as $

1. For example, the subconscious mind needs clear and specific objectives. $ 1 increase also can be said richer. Goals Should be Written Objectives must be written with pen and on paper. Unknowingly we've activated Reticular Active System (RAS) in our brains. RAS is like a missile that serves the pursuit

of objectives and to correct our steps if we get in to the wrong directions. Given that money is actually not the final goal but a means to achieve other goals, we must be clear in determining what the money will be used for. Examples of what can be achieved if we have money:

1. Flexibility to have the things we want both consumptive things such as houses, cars, televisions, furniture, mobile phones and others. Or productive things such as house rent, car rent, boarding houses, wallet bird house and businesses that get the highest money.

2. Flexibility to do things such as: vacations abroad, and other sports. Concerning the financial aspect, for

example, you can specify the destination steady with:

1. Define clearly what goals you want to have and what you want to do with your money.

2. Sets the amount of money you need and when you'll have it. Especially, you need to set the amount of passive income you need and when you will have it.

3. Choose the type of business that allows you to have a passive income or a business that was originally active income that can you invest on thus it can be a passive income. Many people do things they do not like and could not produce what they want. The principle in choosing a business is to choose what

we like and can produce the things we wanted.

Achieving Objectives

We will not act to achieve the goal if we do not feel the need. All tremendous achievement certainly achieved because the person has a very strong reason to be great consciously or not. All the dramatic changes in our lives are also motivated by the desire to achieve pleasure and avoid pain. If we want to change, we must clearly know what kind of misery if we will face if we don't want to change or we don't achieve. We also need to know what joy when we change or achieve it.

There are some things that can be done to feel the need to achieve our goals.

1. Know the disadvantages and advantages.

2. Experienced sufferings and pleasures. Experiencing losses and profits We will feel the need to achieve our goals with the guidance of questions to determine damages if we do not reach it and its advantages when we reach it.

Question:

1. What harm (to be emotionally) will it brings if I did not work to achieve this goal? What will happen to the people I love if I do not work to achieve my goals? What kind of disappointment that they would say to me? Five, ten, twenty years from now on, what will I regret if I do not work to achieve this goal?

2. What's in it (to be emotionally) if I work to achieve this goal? Joy what happened to the people I love that I

worked to achieve my goal? Five years, ten years, twenty years from now, what joy will I get if I worked to achieve my goal?

3. Why do I have to act now to achieve my goal? What will I lose if I procrastinate it? What's in it for me if I do now?

We may feel the need when we are experiencing a painful thing because we did not act towards our goals and imagine the pleasure that should come as a result. The painful experience will change our lives if we learn to give meaning that makes us stronger. So that, it will push us to act towards what we want. Painful experience can be experienced directly or imagined with feeling. Our brains can't differentiate direct experience with the imagine experience if we are emotionally attached in it.

Afterwards, the painful experience will change us and motivate us to act. We will be able to feel the need to achieve our goals when we can feel the pleasure that arises when we have achieved that goal. Imagine the relief you feel when you can make the financial of your family free.

As miserable and pleasures are relative to each person, write one of your goals, then:

1. Imagine, feel the agony with detail and emotion when you do not achieve the goals on the specific time that you set.

2. Imagine, feel and enjoy with intense detail and emotion when you reach the goal on the specific time that you set.

Reason or Unreason

It maybe not makes sense, but when we have a very strong reason and feel compelled to reach these goals, we will find the way. For example, some inventors in the past. They used to see their objectives to invent technology such as air plane, electricity, lamp, and etc... as impossible. Look, today their objectives had become reality. Often, finding a way to achieve what we want is as simple as finding a strong reason why these goals should be achieved. Finding a very strong reason is as simple as finding our ability and willingness to imagine, feel and listening the pleasure in extreme detail and emotionally when we reach our destination or even the pain when we do not reach our goals.

Wealth Creation Strategies

We will take advantage of the added value and leverage to create wealth that gives us well-being, which means "able to survive with the existing styles if tomorrow stop working." Money is a medium of exchange of value added. To put it thoroughly about added value, pay attention to the following sentence. Honesty is an added value. If all people is being honest, then honesty is no longer added value. Long story short, something could be categorized as added value if not everyone has or offer it.

The formula to earn a lot of money is: Added values x Leverage Leverage in question is a tool to facilitate or accelerate the achievement of objectives. Here are a few things that can be given leverage:

1. Resources.

2. Idea.

3. Contact.

4. Expertise So, we do not need to use our own capital, our own ideas, our own contacts and our own expertise.

How to leverage:

1. Asking, proposing, communicating more to the right people so they can give us help and conveniences we need.

2. Use the multiplier factor and not the summer. How to Get Rich Quickly There are several ways that can get us rich quickly.

1. Make money that chase us.

2. Utilize the multiplier factor.

Make Money Chasing Us There are five elements to make money chasing us.

1. Having added value Here is an example to explain more about it: There are two salesmen selling toothpaste. They wanted to offer it to a shop. Salesman A said to the shopkeeper, "Toothpaste brand A is healthier, making your teeth white, and having a cheap price." Meanwhile, the salesman B and told the owner of the shop, "Toothpaste brand B is healthier, making your teeth white, having low prices with bonus buy 10 get 1 free. It's clear that salesman B have added value, which is a bonus of buy 10 get 1 free.

2. Communicating the added value

Although we have added value, but if it is not communicated, people will not know about it. If people do not know, hence the development of your business will be very slow. Many people who have business with products or services that have added value compared to others but tend to not communicate either through sale or by any other means. As a result, the product or service was not a hard sell. Do it like Salesman B promotes his brand added value.

3. Remember your target market.

When we already have products or services that have added value, added value shall be communicated to the right people. There is no point in having added value if we communicate it to people who are not the target market of the product or service. There is no point of selling luxury cars to beggars on the roadside. Although the cars come with added value, they will be difficult to sell.

4. Communicate in significant amounts
If we communicate to the right people, there is bigger chance that people will to want to buy our product or services. But, if our communication is done one by one, it will be a very long process. If you want money chasing you, you should communicate your added value to the right people in large numbers.

5. Keep it appropriate.

All the effort to communicate the added value should be done in proper promotion at the right time and in the right place. There are four external elements that can make everyone get rich, they are: 1. It was lucky that we all have differences in each of us. This matter lies only on how to utilize it.

2. Multiplication which creates an exponential growth. Already, we've had it since we decided to use it.

3. The right choice. We'll have it when we learn to assess more effectively.

4. It I true that we need some amount of money to harvest money. Even more, we also must put up money. Money also follows the principles of rice planting. If you expect to double the harvest, we must sow the seeds folding.

Therefore, we have to start collecting money from now to be planted or invested. Explore profitable business ideas If we see the floor, we'll see ceramic tiles. Ceramic tiles make the people who involved in the process of the making, distributing, and marketing richer. For example, people who install tiles, people who make and sell the ingredients in making ceramic tiles. Another example, when we see the example someone's hair. That hair cans making some groups of people richer. Those people can be the person who sells shampoo, sells a comb, makes shampoo, makes comb, barber, artisan shampooing, and hair accessories traders and so on. A lot of rich people also come from this very field, which is hair. Basically, people looking for money by:

1. Producing required goods or services.

2. Become a supplier of goods or services producer.

3. Become a distributor of produced goods or services.

4. Provide tools to produce goods or services.

5. Teaching about the knowledge of production or service.

6. Become a provider of transportation equipment.

7. Lease the land for manufacturers, suppliers, consumers.

8. Realtor in between everything.

9. Be employees among them all I hope from this day there is no one who runs out of ideas to make money. Recognizing and Utilizing Trends Related with the business idea, it is important that we pay attention and utilizing trend. Trend is something that is growing very rapidly. When we move against the trend, it is like we like against the stream of the river currents. Thus, we will be swept away by the current. For example, do you still want to make a rental video tape? If you are so desperate to make a video tape rental business, it is almost certain that your business will be failed. Currently, video tape technology has been defeated by the technology of VCD player in just 4 years.

Later technology has moved to DVD and currently moving into the era of HDTV or blue ray and so on. We can identify trends in several ways:

1. Analyzing the age and number of people, the amount of income and expenditures.

2. Observing the speed of penetration of a business to society.

3. Seeing trends that occurred outside of the country.

4. Answering the existing problems.

5. Combining two or more good things
6. Improving something that is already good.

7. Change or add something that already exists.

Protecting Your Wealth

The world is changing rapidly and a lot of things keep being replaced by things that completely new. It's just like video tape that developed almost 100 years of time to dominate the market for several years. But after 4 years dominating, the technology of video tape then defeated by the technology of VCD. As a major change of the world trend develops, to be able to survive we need a strong effort to always learn and have an open mind, especially for the wealthy and victorious. Thus, we are required to keep learning and opening our minds to whatever happens in the world.

We are required to learn from the best in the world. When the times change, we must continue to learn to be able to change, following or even leading the development of civilization. To be able to do that, there are several ways to learn:

1. Learn from the experience. Learning from experience is the most memorable learning process. We will remember better when we are experiencing.

2. Learn through the process of analysis, thought and concludes If only counting on the experience, people will never reach the moon. To learn something that is completely new, another process is required. In that case, the thought process begins by comparing something that we receive with our senses with something that already exists in our brain. Then, the

second process we will ask what this means.

3. Learn directly from a mentor or mentors. This is the most quick and easy. For example: We use 80% of our time to study to learn from the best people in the field that we wish to learn, either through seminars, workshops, formal or informal guidance, in friendship. Then we allocate 20% of the time to study any field including the areas that we do not like to open our minds.

4. Learning indirectly from books, tapes, internet and others. This is a way of learning that makes us get the most. Everyone has their own learning style that is most effective. We've heard many times that the mind is like a

parachute. It will be useful for us if it is open. Open our minds by listening to the experiences of successful people that you can earn by way of attending to seminars, listening to tapes and reading book. If we want to learn and become an expert on a certain field, you can do the following steps: - Learn from the best - Learn something completely - Do repetitions with some breaks Building Money Farm Breeding money means the result of investment is sufficient to finance our lifestyles. This investment could be a business that produced with or without us. It can also be royalties on copyright, contracted or rented homes as boarding houses, stocks that generate dividends, mutual funds, Rent house, and others.

There are three principles to build money farm:

1. Delaying pleasure A research is done by collecting children aged 5-6 years in a room. They have been given chocolate candy for each in front of them. They've been told that they may eat chocolate directly. Or, if they want to wait 30 minutes, they will get 2 chocolate candies. The result shows that there are some who wants to wait and some who don't. The most interesting thing is 30 years later, they who wanted to wait 30 minutes were got success faster. The principle of delaying pleasure can be done in three ways: - Wait until we have enough passive income to pay our consumer goods. - Wait until we have the money at least 10 times greater

than the price of luxury goods we want and buy new. - Decreases the pleasure, for example, we were to buy a BMW 7-series but we decided to buy a BMW 5 Series.

2. The asset allocation System of our asset allocation is - Providing a certain amount (percentage) of revenue and income into a safe investment.

3. Providing a certain amount (percentage) of revenue and income into reserves of at least 5-6 months of living expenses. After covering for 5-6 months of living expenses, use a certain percentage of our revenues for growing investment. Spend the rest the percentage of asset allocation depends on several things:

1. The amount of income.

2. The amount of expenditures.

3. The amount of determination to be financially independent the greater our determination to be financially independent, we will further reduce costs, increase revenue and invest the difference into a safe investment and growth. To realize immediately your money farm, no matter what your income you must do the following steps:

1. Allocate minimum 10% of your income for safe investment.

2. Allocate at least 20% of your income, allocated for the investment made 5-6 months living expenses or invested in growing investment.

3. Maximum of 70% of the income spent to meet the needs.

Better Investing

1. Allocate the money in a safe investment that should not be taken.

2. If anything happens and we need cash while our reserve money has been used, it remains a safe investment should not be taken. The interest or the results are not to be taken too. Borrowing money is better to be done on that situation because we will be motivated to return it.

3. When the safe allocation can be taken? It should not be taken at any cost.

4. Interest or the results of asset allocation in the form of safe investments may be taken and used

when the interest or the result of it is enough to fund the living cost.

5. The allocation of pleasure There are two types of people who have the wrong attitude toward money and pleasure. The first type they were so extravagant to enjoy the pleasures of life and mortgaging their future with the principle of enjoy now pay later or have a mortgage now so that their life is never finished paying the debt. The second type is them who are so frugal, stingy and never enjoy the pleasures of life. This makes people divinize money, because the money was never used and only worshiped. They'll never enjoy their wealth to death.

There is no way to live better than by allocating pleasure when we've orderly delayed pleasure and discipline do asset allocation. Multiple Streams of Income (MSI) There is no prohibition to anyone if the person has more than one source of income. Unfortunately, not many people think about it seriously and try hard to get it. Whereas, having more than one source of income is generally better and more secure than only having one. Actually, if you are saving money in the bank you already have more than one income. They are the money you make plus the bank interest. There are some common mistakes that people make about MSI. The first mistake people considering MSI as work and asked; "If I have a job from 8 am to 5 pm do I still have to work from 6 pm until 12 o'clock at night?" MSI is not the job. It is something that continuously make money without having to be involved. The second mistake was busy developing the MSI but do not have a PSI (Primary Stream of Income).

As if a tree, PSI is the trunk. So, it must exist. Before developing MSI, we need to focus on something that we like and making money. After having a steady PSI, then we develop MSI.

The ideal MSI is:

1. Low-Risk.

2. Low Time Involvement.

3. Low Capital.

4. Low Personal Funding.

5. Low Labor

6. Big Thinking.

7. High Returns.

8. Quality Service.

9. Personal Enjoyment.

10. High Growth.11. Unique

12. Easily Duplicatable.

13. High Speed.

Know Thyself

By knowing the natural and easy path will get us rich in a quicker way. According to Roger Hamilton diagram, there are some types of people's natural pathway.

1. Mechanical Types: This type of person likes to rely on and follow the system to become rich. Ray Kroc, MC Donald owner, for example. Although he did not invent the hamburger, he was the one who figured out how to market hamburger extraordinary. That's how McDonalds grow rapidly until now. The characteristics of these types of people prefer to detail and diligent in following the system.

2. Creator Types: The person who belongs to this category is a person who likes creating new things and became rich because of new things. This kind of people is pretty much like the founder of Apple, Steve Jobs, and inventor of computer, Pixar studio, or inventor of the iPod. The characteristics of people are creative, innovative, like new things and like new challenges.

3. Star Types: These person gets rich because it relies on its abilities or special talent that hard to imitate or to duplicate. This category is best represented by people like Mike Tyson, the boxer, and Celine Dion, the singer. The characteristics of the people are having particularly prominent talent, having the expertise to attract

attention, happy to be the center of attention and very stand out in the field.

4. Supporting Types: These people get rich because of its expertise to support or mobilize and organize supporting resources to achieve a goal. Example: Jack Welch (former CEO of General electric). The person who belongs to this group usually has very prominent leadership and managerial capacity.

5. Deal Maker Type: The person who is deal maker acquired to have skill to negotiate and reconcile the two interests or more, for example Li Ka Sing the property tycoons in Hongkong. This type of persons usually has a lot of friends, loves to hang out, is good at convincing people, and happy to match people.

6. Trader Types: This person gets rich because of its ability to sell things or services, just like George Soros. Many people thought that George Soros is an investor, but he is not. He is a true merchant. People like him is usually time sensitive, thorough, no shame in selling, profit-oriented and likes fast or short-term profits.

7. Accumulator Types: This kind of people gets rich by investing without engaging in everyday business, without having the business as a whole, just like Warren Buffet. He is the richest stock investor in the world.

The characteristics of people like him are good and like to analyze numbers, has leadership, pleased to observe trends, like behind the scenes activities, patient, not emotional, and like long-term profitability.

8. Lord Type: This person earns wealth by having a lot of business, for example Liem Sioe Liong the former conglomerate. The characteristics of such people are like calculation, able to see opportunities anywhere, able to delegate, smart in selecting and judging people. For active PSI where we must get a massive income, we must choose a suitable line of business and in accordance with the most natural path for us. In all areas of business or profession we could do it in accordance with the most natural path for us. For example, in health, you can be a star as a doctor who appeared on TV in a health show. In other ways, you can be a

creator by becoming a researcher, inventor of the drug or the founder of the clinic. You can also be a lord by having dispensaries, clinics, midwifery schools and so forth. As a doctor can also be a mechanical person by creating systems and rely on the system to open a network of clinics.

As supporting type, a person can be the head of the hospital, or be a deal maker who bridges the investor for the hospital with the founder of the hospital. Even someone who is trader type can take part in health field by becoming medicine merchant. While an accumulator can be the investor of a hospital, clinic or health laboratories. Rather than focusing on improving our weaknesses, it is better to focus on our strengths and delegate our weaknesses to the best people in their field.

www.ingramcontent.com/pod-product-compliance
Lightning Source LLC
Chambersburg PA
CBHW071305170526
45165CB00003B/1422